Around the World

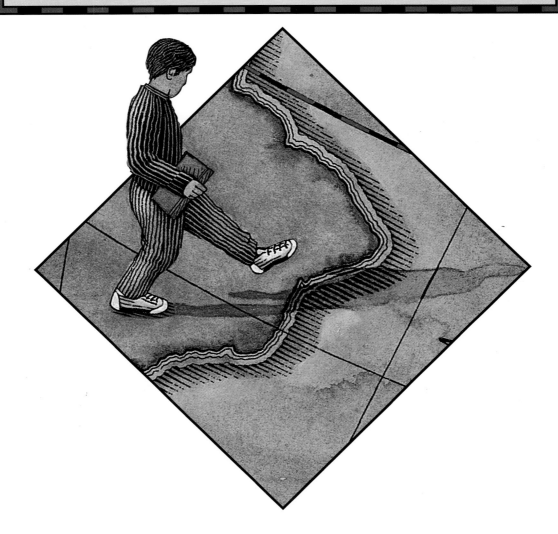

PRENTICE HALL REGENTS

A VIACOM COMPANY

Getting Ready to Read

dinner	plate
food	bowl
cook	cup
taste	pot
eat	pan
nutrition	table
diet	silverware
healthy	spoon
balanced	fork
house	knife
family	chopsticks
neighbor	sour
friend	sweet
delicious	spicy
dish	salty
dishes	

1 Describe dinner time in these three homes.

2 How about your family? How do you cook and eat dinner?

Look at the map. See how people eat rice around the world. How do you like your rice?

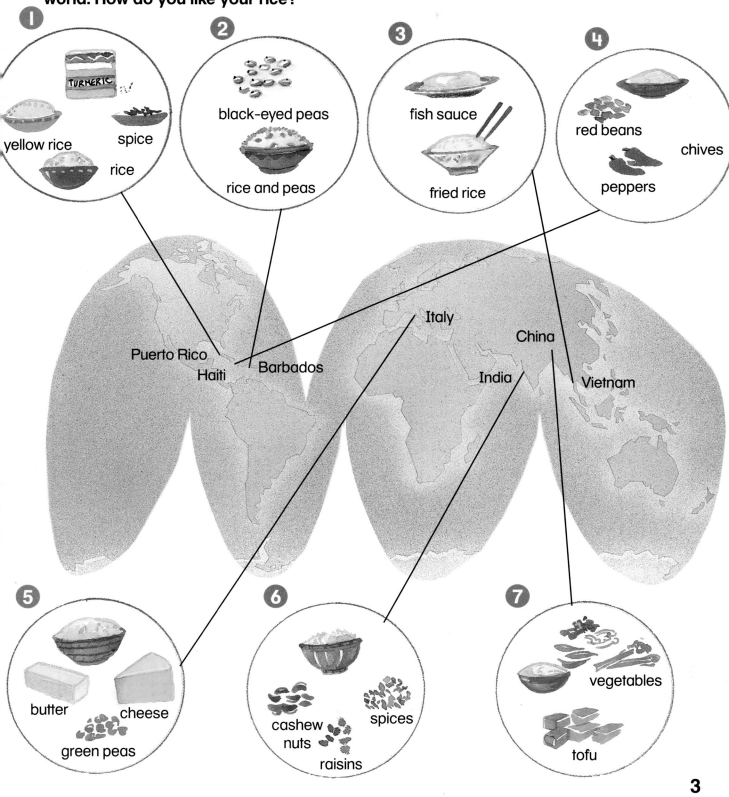

1. yellow rice · spice · rice · TURMERIC
2. black-eyed peas · rice and peas
3. fish sauce · fried rice
4. red beans · chives · peppers
5. butter · cheese · green peas
6. cashew nuts · spices · raisins
7. vegetables · tofu

Puerto Rico · Haiti · Barbados · Italy · China · India · Vietnam

Everybody Cooks Rice

by Norah Dooley

My stomach was grumbling. Mom was cooking dinner, and I couldn't wait to sit down and eat. "Carrie, will you go out and find Anthony—dinner is almost ready."

Mom is always asking me to look for Anthony. He's my little brother, and he's such a moocher! If he's not playing ball or hopscotch, he's at a neighbor's house tasting their dinner.

I walked outside and looked up and down the street. I couldn't see Anthony anywhere, so I went over to Mrs. Darlington's house. Anthony and I call her Mrs. D. She's our next-door neighbor.

Mr. and Mrs. D. are from Barbados. It was Thursday, so their grandchildren, Sean and Stephanie, were over having their favorite dinner—black-eyed peas and rice. At the front door I could smell fried onions and bacon. It made my mouth water. I ate a small cup of rice and black-eyed peas while Mr. D. told stories about Barbados. People swim there and go fishing—even in December!

Suddenly I remembered I was supposed to be looking for Anthony, so I asked if anyone had seen him. Sean said he'd seen Anthony going into the Diazes' house. I went there next.

When I walked into the kitchen, my friend Fendra Díaz and her little brother, Tito, were cooking dinner because their mom was working late. Tito was telling Fendra that she uses too much spice. Fendra said Tito was checking the pot too often, so the rice and pigeon peas would never cook. Their teenage brother, José, told them to pipe down. He wanted to watch TV.

I looked in the pot to see what was cooking. The rice was bright yellow! Fendra told me that her grandmother in Puerto Rico had taught her how to cook with turmeric. Turmeric makes rice yellow. Tito gave me a taste from the cooking spoon. Boy, was it delicious! Then I asked if anyone had seen Anthony. Fendra said Anthony had been there to taste their dinner but had left to visit Dong. So I went across the street to Dong's house.

Dong Tran came from Vietnam five years ago with his whole family—aunts, uncles, cousins, and all. Dong's older sister, Tam, answered the door. Mr. and Mrs. Tran work late every day, so everyone else takes turns making dinner. It was Tam's turn to cook. She was busy making the garlicky, fishy sauce, called *nuoc cham*. She let me try it on some rice. It was sweet and salty and sour. It tasted…interesting. Later when Mrs. Tran gets home, she'll make fried rice with peas. Then when Mr. Tran gets home, everyone will sit down and eat together.

When I asked if anyone had seen my brother, Dong said Anthony had been helping Mrs. Hua and Mei-Li with their groceries. The Huas live on the corner so I started to walk up the street.

"Carrie, wait up!" someone called. It was my friend Rajit. He was carrying three round metal boxes all clipped together. Something inside smelled delicious, so I asked him what it was. Rajit said his parents were working at their video and gift shop, so he was bringing them leftovers in a tiffin carrier.

There was a big party at the Krishnamurthy's house last weekend, so Rajit's mother cooked a fancy, colorful Indian dish called *biryani*. It's made with peas, cashews, raisins, lots of spices, and a special kind of rice called basmati rice. I had tasted *biryani* at Rajit's house the last time I went out looking for Anthony.

When I told Rajit that I was looking for my brother *again,* he said Anthony and Mei-Li were blowing bubbles out a window of the Huas' house.

The Huas came from China a year ago. Mrs. Hua is just learning how to speak English. We smile at each other a lot.

Mrs. Hua was steaming white rice for her family and the boarder who lives in the back room. She was also making tofu and vegetables in the wok—that's a big pan with a round bottom. Mrs. Hua always makes me sit down and eat something when I come over.

Everyone at the Huas' house uses chopsticks. Mei-Li, who is only three and a half years old, can even pick up a single grain of rice with her chopsticks! Mei-Li laughed at me when I tried using chopsticks and dropped some vegetables. She said Anthony was "bye-bye," so I decided to try our backyard neighbors, the Bleus.

The Bleus are from Haiti. Their cat just had kittens, so Anthony wanders over there a lot. Mrs. Bleu teaches English at the community center. We get to call her Madame Bleu. Madame Bleu speaks three languages—French, English, and Creole.

When I walked in, Madame Bleu was making a creole style Haitian dinner. It had hot peppers, chives, red beans, and you guessed it—rice. Monsieur Bleu works two jobs, so he won't get home till late. Madame Bleu says the pot will stay on the stove, and the rice will get tastier and spicier.

Adeline and Jeanne-Marie Bleu came home for dinner on their break from their after-school jobs at the grocery store. They helped themselves to bowls of rice and beans from the pot, and gave some to me. I thought my mouth was on fire! Jeanne-Marie teased me when I gulped some water.

It was getting late, and I still hadn't found Anthony. Adeline said she had seen him with a kitten in his arms, climbing the fence to our yard. I said thanks and *au revoir*—that means good-bye— and hurried home.

When I walked into the house, Anthony was showing the kitten to our baby sister, Anna. He was explaining to Mom that he was only borrowing the kitten.

Mom was putting dinner on the table. Her grandmother, from northern Italy, taught our grandmother, who taught Mom how to cook *risi e bisi*—rice with green peas. Mom puts butter, grated cheese, and some nutmeg on it. It smelled so good, but my stomach wasn't grumbling anymore. I told Mom that I was too full to eat. Anthony said he wanted to eat his dinner, even though he was full, because he loves rice, and that afternoon he found out that *everybody* cooks rice.

After You Read

Vijay, Kim, Isabelle, and Katrina were busy when the mail came. What was each one doing?

EVERYDAY TALK

- **Making a polite request**
- **Complimenting someone**
- **Asking to be excused**

If you are invited to dinner at a friend's house, what do you say?

MAY I PLEASE HAVE THE POTATOES?

THE DINNER IS DELICIOUS. THANK YOU FOR INVITING ME.

YOU'RE WELCOME. WE'RE GLAD YOU'RE HERE.

MAY WE PLEASE BE EXCUSED?

YES, YOU MAY.

Getting Ready to Read

What games are the people playing? What are the players doing? Which sports do you like to play or watch?

basketball

backboard

basket

jump

goal

goalie

opponents

kick

soccer

baseball

mask

bat

helmet

glove

fielder

umpire

chest protector

batter

pitch
throw

catcher

shin guards

pitcher

table tennis

hit

paddle

balls

volleyball

hit

teammates

net

field hockey

referee

stick

run

15

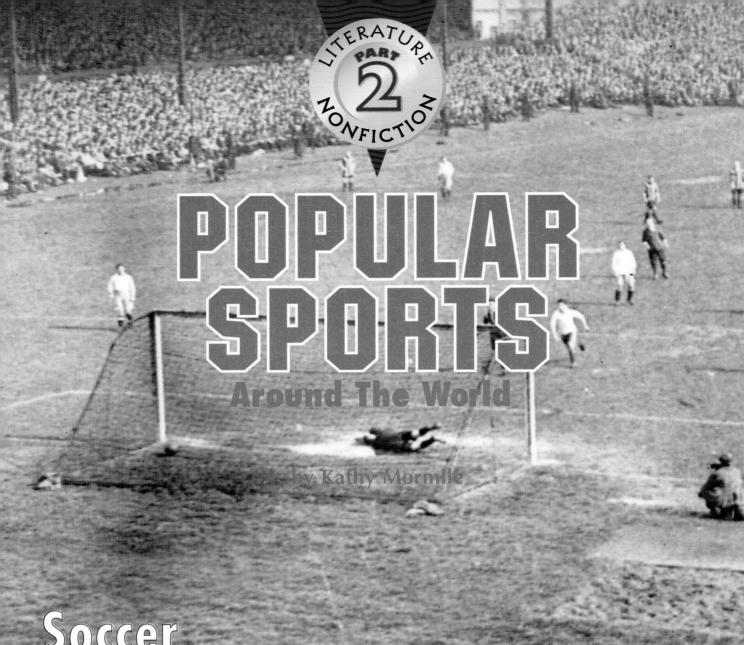

POPULAR SPORTS
Around The World

by Kathy Mormile

Soccer

For centuries, people have been playing kicking games with a ball. The game of soccer developed from some of these early games. The English probably gave soccer its name and its first set of rules. In European countries, soccer is called *football* or *association football.* Some people believe that the name soccer came from "assoc.," an abbreviation for the word *association.* Others believe that the name came from the high socks that the players wear.

Organized soccer games began in 1863. In soccer, two teams of eleven players try to kick or head the ball into their opponents' goal. The goalie, who tries to keep the ball out of the goal, is the only player on the field who may touch the ball with his or her hands. The other players use their feet, heads, and bodies to control the ball.

Every four years, soccer teams around the world compete for the World Cup. World Cup competition started in 1930.

Brazil is the home of many great soccer players, including the most famous player of all, Pelé. With his fast footwork, dazzling speed, and great scoring ability, Pelé played for many years in Brazil and then later in New York. During his 22 years in soccer, he scored 1,281 goals and held every major record.

People in more than 140 countries around the world play soccer. It is the national sport of most European and Latin American countries. Soccer is definitely the world's most popular sport!

Basketball

James Naismith, a physical education teacher in Massachusetts, invented basketball in 1891. Naismith's boss asked him to invent a game that students could play indoors during bad weather. He wanted a game that wasn't as rough as soccer, football, or wrestling. Naismith attached peach baskets to a railing ten feet above the floor at either end of the gym. The players used a soccer ball. A person sat on a ladder at each end and threw out the balls that went into the basket. Naismith decided that having only five players on a team would keep the game from getting too rough. Two years later, metal hoops with net bags replaced the peach baskets. Officials pulled a string on the nets to release the balls that went in. In 1894, he added the backboard, along with a larger ball. In 1913, people began using the bottomless nets we use today.

During a basketball game, two teams of five players each throw the ball into two baskets at opposite ends of a court. Players bounce, or dribble, the ball to the basket or pass the ball to teammates. A team scores points by getting the ball into their team's basket. The team with the highest score wins.

By the mid 1900s, basketball was the most popular indoor sport. Athletes in about 130 countries play the game. Basketball is very popular in the U.S., China, and Puerto Rico.

Baseball

Baseball began in the United States in the early 1800s. Some people believe that Abner Doubleday invented the game. Others think that baseball came from an old British sport called *rounders.* Baseball and rounders are very similar. However, in rounders, the field players throw the ball right at the runner. If the ball hits the runner, he or she is out. In baseball, a field player just *touches* the ball to the base or the running player to get the player out.

Today's baseball players use special equipment to help prevent injuries. Field players wear baseball gloves to protect their hands. The catcher wears a metal mask, a chest protector, and shin guards. Batters wear plastic helmets to protect their heads.

Every spring in the United States, people of all ages play baseball at local baseball fields. Children and adults go to ballparks to see their favorite players and to eat peanuts and hot dogs. It's no wonder that baseball is called the national pastime of the United States.

People in many countries love baseball. The sport is very popular in Cuba, the Dominican Republic, Japan, Puerto Rico, Canada, Italy, Taiwan, the Netherlands, South Africa, and many Latin American nations. One of the greatest baseball players was a Puerto Rican athlete named Roberto Clemente.

Volleyball

Volleyball was invented by William Morgan, another physical education teacher in Massachusetts. He stretched a tennis net across the gym and used the inner lining of a basketball to play his new game. The players used their hands and arms to hit the ball over the net.

Like many sports, volleyball began slowly, but it gradually spread to many different countries. Volleyball became part of the Olympics in 1964. It was during these Olympic games that the skilled Japanese women's team showed the world that volleyball can be a super-fast sport. Today, athletes in more than 150 nations play volleyball.

Table Tennis

Table tennis or Ping-Pong began in Great Britain. It is played on a rectangular table with small wooden paddles and a very light ball. Players hit the ball back and forth over a net that is stretched across the center of the table. Two or four people can play the game.

When the game started, it was called Ping-Pong, a name which suggested the sound the ball makes during the game.

The game's name was later changed to table tennis.

Today, table tennis is extremely popular in China. Many Chinese start at four years old to learn how to play. China, however, is not the only country that has great table tennis players. Table tennis players enjoy the game in over 100 countries around the world.

Field Hockey

Egyptian wall paintings show people holding sticks and hitting a small ball. These paintings suggest that a game like hockey has been played for thousands of years.

Field hockey is like soccer in many ways. In both sports there are eleven players on a team, and the teams try to hit a ball into their opponent's goal. However, in field hockey, the ball is much smaller and the players use curved sticks to move the ball.

In the early years of hockey, players were allowed to swing their sticks any way they wanted, and many were injured. Today players may not raise their sticks above shoulder level. This rule has helped reduce the number of injuries.

In the United States, field hockey is a popular women's sport. In other countries, only men play the game. Field hockey is especially popular in India and Pakistan.

After You Read

What is wrong with this picture? How would you correct the mistakes?

Create your own sport! Think about these questions. Then draw a picture and write five things about your new sport.

- Is it a team or individual sport?
- Is it an indoor or outdoor sport?
- How many players will be on a team?
- What is the object of the game?
- What are the rules of the game?
- How do players score?

PART 3

JUST for FUN

A MAGAZINE FOR KIDS

Best Supermarket

Fresh VEGETABLES

Lettuce
89¢
each

Tomatoes
69¢ per pound

Onions
$2.39
per 2 lb. bag

Green Peppers
4 for $1

Special!

1 lb. box **98¢**

Uncle Sam's
Long Grain
Rice

YUMMY
BRAND
BLACK-EYED PEAS

4 lb. bag
$2.69

MAX'S CANNED WHOLE TOMATOES

1 lb. can
89¢

12 oz. box
SALT
79¢

4 oz. bottle
for
$2.89

BAY LEAVES
$1.99 2 oz. bottle

Read the food ads.
Read the recipe card.
About how much
would it cost to buy
the ingredients to
make Spanish-
American rice?

Spanish-American Rice

1 onion, sliced	¼ c. olive oil	1 c. water
½ green pepper, seeded and chopped fine	1 c. rice	1 tsp. salt
	1 lb. can tomatoes	1 bay leaf

1. Cook onion and green pepper in oil until soft.
2. Add rice and stir.
3. Add tomatoes, water, salt, and bay leaf. Cover and bring to a boil.
4. Lower heat and cook 20 minutes or until water is absorbed.

Serves 4 people

SPORTS NEWS

Read the newspaper headlines. Which article would you read first? Why?

Girls' Soccer Competition Set for Weekend

Ping-Pong Championship Tonight

Basketball Team Nets Win

West High School Volleyball Team On the Ball

What do the sports tables tell you?

Which teams are winning?

Which teams do you like?

NFL STANDINGS				
American Conference				
Team	W*	L*	T*	Pct.*
EAST				
Miami	8	4	0	.667
N.Y. Jets	6	6	0	.500
Buffalo	6	6	0	.500
New England	6	6	0	.500
Indianapolis	5	7	0	.417
CENTRAL				
Pittsburgh	9	3	0	.750
Cleveland	9	3	0	.750
Cincinnati	2	10	0	.167
Houston	1	11	0	.083
WEST				
San Diego	9	3	0	.750
Kansas City	7	5	0	.583
Denver	6	6	0	.500
L.A. Raiders	6	6	0	.500
Seattle	5	7	0	.417

National Conference				
Team	W*	L*	T*	Pct.*
EAST				
Dallas	10	2	0	.883
Philadelphia	7	5	0	.583
N.Y. Giants	5	7	0	.417
Arizona	5	7	0	.417
Washington	2	10	0	.167
CENTRAL				
Chicago	8	5	0	.615
Minnesota	8	5	0	.615
Green Bay	6	6	0	.500
Detroit	6	6	0	.500
Tampa Bay	3	9	0	.250
WEST				
San Francisco	9	2	0	.818
Atlanta	6	6	0	.500
New Orleans	4	7	0	.364
L.A. Rams	4	8	0	.333

*W=Wins, L=Losses, T=Ties, Pct.=Win/Loss Percent

TODAY'S CROSSWORD

Across
1. Balls used in the national pastime
4. You can cook rice in a _____ .
5. 2
6. In table tennis, players hit a ball over a _____ .
8. Everybody cooks _____ .
10. Dish
12. Catchers wear a _____ to help them catch the ball.
13. Opposite of a daughter

Down
1. Some people put this on bread.
2. Rice and _____
3. Where we buy things
7. We eat dinner at the _____ .
9. Makes something to eat
11. 10

EVERYDAY TALK

- **Extending an invitation**
- **Accepting/declining an invitation**

SORRY, BUT I HAVE TO DO MY HOMEWORK. THANKS ANYWAY.

ROGER, WOULD YOU LIKE TO GO TO THE FIELD HOCKEY GAME WITH ME?

DO YOU WANT TO GO TO MY SISTER'S FIELD HOCKEY GAME?

I WISH I COULD, BUT I'M SICK. MAYBE ANOTHER TIME.

HOW WOULD YOU LIKE TO GO TO THE FIELD HOCKEY GAME, DAD?

GREAT IDEA! LET'S GO!

Read the cartoon strip. Then try this conversation with a friend:

Student 1:   Would you like to go to _____ with me?
Student 2:   Sorry, but I have to _____.
             Thanks anyway.

Now try this conversation:

Student 1:   Invite two friends to dinner at your hous___
Student 2:   Say you can't go and explain why not.
Student 3:   Accept the invitation.

Let's Eat!

People in different countries eat in different ways. In the United States, people use knives, forks, and spoons. In China, Japan, and other Asian countries, people eat with chopsticks and flat–bottomed soup spoons. Some people in India and North Africa use the fingers of their right hand. What do you use when you eat at home? Which utensils are used in your home country?

Theme Project

It's almost time for the Multicultural Lunch.
Is everything ready? Here's a checklist.

1 Have you invited your guests? Have they responded?

2 Do you know what food each family is bringing?

3 What decorations will you put up?

4 Who will set up?

5 What dishes and utensils will you use? Do you have them yet?

6 Who will greet the guests?

7 Who will clean up?

Discuss all your plans and get ready to have fun at the lunch!

Theme Activities

Find the Pictures!

This family is shopping for dinner. What else will they need? Look closely at the picture to find these hidden things:

bowl	spoon	cup	fork	chopsticks
table	soy sauce	oil	knife	vegetables

Match the Headlines!

Local Team Wins Tournament Final

Home Team Loses

Star Player Saves the Day!

Player Trips; Team Out of Play-offs

Choose a headline for each photo. Which one is left over?

Prentice Hall Regents
Publisher: Marilyn Lindgren
Project Editors: Carol Callahan, Kathleen Ossip
Assistant Editor: Susan Frankle
Director of Production: Aliza Greenblatt
Manufacturing Buyer: Dave Dickey
Production Coordinator: Ken Liao
Marketing Manager: Richard Seltzer

McClanahan & Company, Inc.
Editorial, Design, Production and Packaging
Project Director: Susan Cornell Poskanzer
Creative Director: Lisa Olsson
Design Director: Toby Carson
Director of Production: Karen Pekarne

PRENTICE HALL REGENTS
A VIACOM COMPANY

© 1996 by Prentice Hall Regents
Prentice Hall, Inc.
A Viacom Company
Upper Saddle River, NJ 07458

Printed in the United States of America

10 9 8 7 6 5 4 3 2 1

ISBN 0-13-349770-4

Prentice-Hall International (UK) Limited, London
Prentice-Hall of Australia Pty. Limited, Sydney
Prentice-Hall Canada Inc., Toronto
Prentice-Hall Hispanoamerican, SA., Mexico
Prentice-Hall of India Private Limited, New Delhi
Prentice-Hall of Japan, Inc., Tokyo
Simon & Schuster Asia Pte. Ltd., Singapore
Editora Prentice-Hall do Brasil, Ltda., Rio de Janeiro

Acknowledgments

Grateful acknowledgment is made to the following publishers, authors, and agents for their permission to reprint copyrighted material. The following literature appears in both Teacher's and Student Books:

Carolrhoda Books, Inc.: *Everybody Cooks Rice* by Norah Dooley. Illustrated by Peter Thornton. Copyright © 1991 by Carolrhoda Books, Inc, used by permission of the publisher. All rights reserved.

Cover
Brian Callanan

Photography
Archive Photos p18–19, p20–21; Bettman Archive p16–17, p19 (left); Culver Pictures p24; Focus on Sports p23 (inset); Orro Greule/Allsport p22 (all); International Table Tennis Federation p23; Janeart Ltd./Image Bank p31 (center); Ken Karp Photography p28 (bottom), p29; Mitchell B. Reibel/Sports Photo Masters p17 (left); Sports Photo Masters p21 (left); Al Tielemans/Duomo p24 (inset); David Young-Wolff/Photoedit p31 (top, bottom)

Illustration
Joe Boddy p31 (top); Gwen Connelly p2–3, p13 (top); Rachel Geswaldo p26 (tomatoes), p27, p31 (bottom right); Paul Meinel p26–27; Steve Sanford p14–15, p25; Peter Spacek p30; Ron Zalme p13 (bottom), p28 (top)